WHAT
MEN
SHOULD
UNDERSTAND
ABOUT
WOMEN

Nancy Van Pelt

First published 2009

© 2009
Reprinted 2010, 2011 and 2014

All rights reserved. No part of this publication may be reproduced in any form without prior permission from the publisher.

British Library Cataloguing in Publication Data. A catalogue record for this book is available from the British Library.

ISBN 978-1-906381-49-3

Published by Autumn House, Grantham, Lincolnshire.

Printed in China.

First up:
A woman
craves
affection.

Affection is central to a woman's relationship with her husband. Without affection a woman feels distant, disconnected and eventually totally alienated from her mate.

For a woman affection symbolises emotional security. When a husband showers his wife with affection he says all over again, 'You are important to me. I will always take care of you and protect you. You can count on me to be concerned about what concerns you. I'll always be there for you.'

A hug – with no sexual overtones – is one way of filling a woman's need for affection.

If the hug includes grasping and grabbing, a woman begins to think a husband has sex, not affection, on his mind. In *his* mind the two are closely connected; not so for her.

Affection must precede sex for the woman.

The first step to becoming more affectionate is to learn as much as you can about the emotional needs of your wife.

If that is a problem for you, ask your wife how she would most like to have you show affection. Better than anyone else, she knows what displays of affection would be the most meaningful.

Practise being affectionate.

Don't build your wife's hopes with good intentions and then not follow through.

Are you not naturally affectionate or demonstrative?

You *can* be! It may take time for affectionate behaviour to come naturally or become a habit without conscious thought, but now is the time to make a start.

Begin with affectionate gestures which are easiest for you and then move to the ones you find a little less natural. Don't give up when a new habit is difficult. The more you practise, the easier a behaviour will become.

Eventually you will enjoy meeting your wife's needs for affection. She will love and appreciate you more and you'll both be winners.

Some ideas on how to be affectionate:

- Write her a love note and tape it to the bathroom mirror.

- Surprise her with a gift for no reason.

- Use a thoughtful
  message to invite
  her for a dinner date
  at a special restaurant.

- Present her with a
  bouquet of flowers
  and enclose a card.

- Tell her how nice her hair looks, or how pretty her eyes are, or how lovely . . .

- Give her a hug and kiss before you get out of bed in the morning.

- Smile and wink at her.

- Give her a hug and kiss when you come home at night.

- Ask her to go for a walk with you after dinner.

- Give her a foot rub.

A woman needs to talk to feel close.

Men would do well to understand the female need to talk about feelings and problems.

When a woman talks,
she is usually not
seeking advice,
solutions or answers.

She is simply exploring her
feelings. When this exploration
is cut off, it short-circuits the
process and she feels alienated
from her mate.

A woman talks in a search for intimacy to gain her partner's empathy and understanding, as she would with her women friends.

A man can make a
real impact on a
woman – by simply
listening to her, without
interrupting, without
offering advice.

A woman talks about problems to feel better. She talks about present problems, problems that may never happen and unsolvable problems. It helps to relieve her stress.

When a woman feels she is heard, she feels validated, listened to and cared about. Even though the problems are still there, her stress level goes down.

A woman also discusses the problems of her family and friends. *This is normal female behaviour.*

She is expressing her care and concern. She is thinking out loud.

Putting her thoughts and feelings into words allows a woman's intuition to kick in.

When a woman shares upset feelings or verbalises problems, a man mistakenly assumes that she is seeking expert advice. He has trouble understanding why, after he has tried to solve things for her, she gets more upset.

A tactic confusing to men is the female tendency to give volumes of detail. A male struggles to find the relevance of the detail to the problem. As she talks, he searches for the bottom line so he can formulate a solution.

He has missed the point.

A woman wants to talk about more than the children and bills. She wants to tell her partner all her 'secrets' and have him listen. . . .

If a man does not listen
she may get back at
him by provoking
an argument over
nothing. . . .

Just listen.

In most cases the woman is not trying to win the argument. She only wants to feel that you hear her and care about her.

Your wife wants to have a relationship sufficiently free so that she can talk with you about the trivia of life that hurts or displeases her, the everyday happenings, what she did and said, the children's successes and failures, worries over a parent's health.

When a woman feels she has been listened to, she feels validated and accepted.

When your wife feels listened to, she experiences an intimacy and closeness that goes beyond her wildest dreams. You will not only be her lover, but her dearest friend and companion.

A woman needs honesty, openness and trust.

When a woman cannot trust her man to give her accurate information about what he is doing with his time and his money (or anything else) she has no basis for a relationship with him.

Trust is foundational to making marriage work.

Without honesty and trust there can be no openness between the couple and every conversation will be inhibited.

Men in the habit of 'fibbing', fabricating stories or distorting the truth – had better change their ways!

Some men lie to 'protect' their wives from unpleasant realities. They tell their wives everything is fine to keep the peace.

But consider the cost:

The man is irritable, depressed and moody and his wife can't figure out why.

She will need to know the truth sooner or later, so it had better be now.

When a man communicates openly and truthfully with his wife, he contributes to her emotional security. If he is truthful, even when a crisis hits, he knows in advance she can handle it.

A woman needs the facts in order to know how to adjust to the situation and stand by her husband's side. Game-playing and evasion of truth are bad ideas.

When one partner has had an affair, the relationship can be rebuilt only through this type of honesty. The couple will need counselling with a qualified counsellor who understands the importance of total honesty once an affair has been confessed.

Confession allows for purging for the guilty party and provides the environment needed to rebuild a stable marriage. But the injured party must regain trust once again.

Disclosure of adultery and other personal problems must be approached on an individual basis. Seek the advice of a professional Christian marital therapist.

A man cannot confess and then immediately demand trust from his wife. Trust cannot be turned on and off like a light.

It is possible to rebuild trust. But over time. Usually a long time. The offending party should provide daily information about his whereabouts, accounting for all activities so that they can easily be verified.

A marriage can survive many setbacks and struggles. But the one thing a marriage cannot survive is a lack of honesty.

PMS: the real story

Premenstrual syndrome is a physiological problem affecting a woman's body, which, in turn, impacts everyone close to her.

Some health professionals list PMS as a primary contributor to marital breakdown. Common problems and struggles are complicated and magnified many times over when PMS strikes.

Ongoing marital
struggles are difficult
enough to endure and
survive when a husband
understands his wife
when PMS strikes.
When a man does
not understand . . .

Both husband and wife
need to understand that
the wife is not crazy
and that it's not all in
her head. They also
need to understand that
there is something they
can do about PMS.

PMS is a physical and psychological disorder that occurs regularly during the same phase of a woman's menstrual cycle (between ovulation and the onset of menstruation), followed by a symptom-free phase.

Common PMS symptoms include fatigue, depression, tension, headaches and mood swings. Other symptoms related to PMS are both psychological and physical. See next page.

Psychological: Anger, sudden mood swings, emotional over-responsiveness, unexplained crying, irritability, anxiety, forgetfulness, decreased concentration.

Physical: Bloating, weight gain, acne, dizziness, migraines, diarrhoea, sweating.

Symptoms occur monthly, generally within 7-14 days prior to menstruation. Symptoms may seem to worsen as menstruation approaches.

PMS symptoms can last for a couple of days to a couple of weeks. Medical experts estimate that up to 80% of all women have had PMS symptoms at some point, but only 8-10% experience symptoms severe enough to require medical treatment.

It can help both husband and wife to cope if they take the trouble to chart the menstrual cycle. This is the best way to determine whether you are dealing with PMS or something else.

Become informed.

Both husband and wife need to find out as much as they can about PMS. Husbands need to accompany their wives to medical appointments.

Eat healthily.

For many PMS
sufferers diet makes
a big difference.

A week or two before the onset of menstruation, a woman can adjust her diet in the following ways:

1. Eliminate sugar.

2. Include whole grains and fresh vegetables and fruit.

3. Avoid salty and smoked foods and dairy products.

There are two more things women can do that may help:

- Exercise regularly. Experts agree that exercise is one of the best treatments for PMS.

- Relax. Meditation, deep breathing, walks, massage, or hot baths also reduce tension.

What husbands can do:

Learn what kind of support your wife wants during this time. Encourage her to walk by walking with her. Give her a break from household chores. Whip up a meal or take her out to eat.

Don't take what happens during her mood swings personally. Recognise that PMS is a normal part of her life and accept it without being devastated by some of the things she says or does.

PMS is the result of both hormone level changes and their interaction with central neurotransmitters, such as serotonin.

Serotonin is a natural chemical in the brain that regulates mood and appetite. Serotonin levels are usually lower than normal during the PMS timeframe.

A woman needs financial security.

Women have a right to expect financial support from their husbands. God ordained that the husband provide for the family.

Many women today work outside the home. Some say they want a career in order to be happy. Some resent working, especially when forced to do so in order to pay basic living expenses.

Husband and wife must be careful not to set a standard of living beyond their needs to be happy.

Happiness can be maximised, in some cases, when families reduce to a smaller but comfortable home, with a husband able to be home with the family more and a wife not needing to work outside the home during critical child-rearing years.

Women should be free to choose a career if they want one. But they should be able to depend on their husband's salary to cover basic living expenses to support the family.

Men must recognise that a woman's need for financial security goes deep into her soul and is vitally connected to the respect she holds for her husband.

A man does not have this need. He finds contentment in providing adequately for the financial needs of his family.

Some men actually resent it or feel threatened when their wives work, especially if their wives earn more than they do! A man usually wants to see himself as the primary wage earner.

A couple should think through what they really *need* rather than what they want. The things we want but don't really need can become our own worst enemy.

Men sometimes work themselves into an early grave trying to provide a standard of living that not only doesn't contribute to marital happiness, but actually brings on stress and disharmony.

Some men naively think that they are driven by love for their wives in overworking to earn more money to live on a grander scale. The truth is that once a woman feels neglected, sensing that her husband puts wealth, status and his job before her, feelings of resentment build.

A woman needs a commitment to family.

A man should recognise that when he commits himself to spending quality time with his children, he automatically strengthens his marriage.

Quality time involves time spent with a child other than in child-care tasks (such as feeding and dressing) in which positive interaction and bonds of love and respect are developed.

What activities might a family engage in to enjoy quality time?

Bike riding, reading aloud to the children before bedtime, attending church, teaching the children about financial planning, family meetings, conducting family worship and engaging the children in religious activities, board games, sporting events, a family project such as building a go-kart.

Family activities demonstrate to the children that it is fun to be together as a family. Show them how co-operation, sharing, respect and encouragement are achieved.

Children under the age of 12 can usually be guided into family activities without a problem. But once children enter their teen years, activities with peers usually take precedence. Parents of teens can only *attempt* to interest their children in well-planned events designed to interest them.

Begin family activities when your children are young, and they will grow up with the concept.

The most important concept a man needs to learn is to work with his wife and not against her in the discipline and training of the children. When a child wants a privilege, it is granted only when Mum and Dad have discussed it in private. . . .

Men get involved in careers, church functions, responsibilities and hobbies. Men prefer working to going home because it satisfies ego needs. Every man needs to sort through his priorities: family first.

The years are slipping
by. Children grow up.
Do your children really
know you, or do they
think of you as the
man who sleeps here
sometimes?

Are changes required?

Does your wife feel neglected? Unless you make some changes, one day you may wake up to find your children grown and your wife gone.

For physiological reasons, men hunger for sexual release more consistently than women.

Women need to be 'in the mood'; and there are many factors that determine this. Among these is the menstrual cycle, the stage of her life in general and how the man behaves in the hours leading up to 'bedtime'.

The male's desire for frequency sharply contrasts with the female's. Not only do men and women differ vastly in desire, but there are also enormous differences between women. Approximately 20% of adult females might be termed 'inhibited', which means that they express a negative or lukewarm attitude towards sex.

The answers to a woman's sexual issues usually lie in what is happening between her and her sexual partner, not what is happening 'in her mind'.

Orgasm capacity in a woman is very strongly tied to her perceptions and feelings concerning the dependability of her relationships with the significant people in her life.

Men and women have the same half-dozen sex hormones, only in differing amounts. It is testosterone that fuels the sex drive in both genders. The fact that men have ten to twenty times more testosterone than women is one of the primary reasons they experience greater desire.

Studies show that some women are more interested in sex during ovulation, when their bodies produce the most testosterone. Other women, particularly those with high testosterone levels, feel sexier just before menstruation. Some appear to be more interested in sex during the first half of the menstrual cycle.

Some studies suggest that a third of all women rarely have enough spontaneous interest in sex to initiate lovemaking. They may enjoy sex and be orgasmic, but they don't experience a pressing physical need to make love as men do.

If either partner has an *unusually* low level of sexual desire they should report for a complete physical examination. If blood tests indicate a hormone deficiency, the individual should be referred to an endocrinologist for further testing and treatment.

Problems arise when there is
a marked difference between
the needs and desires of a
husband and wife.
Compromise is necessary
in order for both to be happy.
When a husband's needs are
stronger than his wife's he
does not have to demand
intercourse at every whim. . . .

Statistics on frequency tend to make us preoccupied with numbers; but studies show that couples in their 20s and 30s have sex on the average of 1-3 times a week. Couples 45 years of age or older report an average of once a week. A new study suggests that *women* in the over-40 age bracket actually wish for more frequent intercourse.

The woman who has a low orgasm capacity is characterised by fear of loss of significant relationships.

She feels that significant people in her life will either go away or let her down. She finds it difficult to trust, to relax, and her apprehension robs her body of its ability to respond sexually.

The clitoris is the centre of a woman's sexual desire. It has no other function than to produce sexual desire. Termed 'the trigger of female desire', it is the most sensitive point for female sexual arousal.

The first evidence of sexual arousal for the female will be lubrication of the vagina. This lubrication takes place within seconds of sexual arousal but is only a beginning sign of arousal *and does not signify that she is ready for or desires intercourse.*

Men need to become skilful in learning to delay the 'point of no return' as long as necessary to satisfy their wives. With practice he can learn to pause prior to the point of no return and relax before crossing over the line.

Gentle, creative, loving touches to a woman's genitalia will be more welcome than a rough, demanding approach.

The loving husband will gently massage the clitoral area until his wife indicates that she is ready for entry.

A couple should engage in love-play that both enjoy. Usually the husband is the more willing to initiate a greater variety of lovemaking experiences, but he should not force these upon an unwilling partner.

A man needs to keep in mind
through the entire process that
his wife is a whole person –
not just a vulva or a clitoris –
and pleasure all of her. Kissing,
breast play and caressing
and fondling of the vulva
and clitoris are what foreplay
is all about.

Orgasm for the female begins with what has been described as a sensation of 'suspension', probably caused by uterine contractions, followed by a wave of warmth that sweeps through her body. The muscle contractions and rushing out of fluids create the sensation of orgasm and an immense sense of pleasure and relief.

Men's bodies return to normal abruptly following sex. Women's do not. It usually takes ten to fifteen minutes. Following orgasm a woman has a subconscious need to remain in touch with her husband. He neglects this need at his peril!

Some couples think that the main goal in intercourse is to reach orgasm simultaneously. Since only 17% of all couples experience a simultaneous orgasm – and even then only on occasion – this leaves many couples wondering whether their sexual experiences are lacking.

Trying to achieve orgasm at the same time can actually make sex less fulfilling.

If the male times it so that the female has her orgasm first, he can then help to intensify it and can fully enjoy her pleasure.

A great sex life means that sometimes sex will be fantastic, and other times only ordinary. But whatever the intensity, it should always be loving.

New research into
female sexuality
has shown that some
women can experience
many orgasms in a
brief period of time.
A continuously
stimulated woman
is capable of five or
more orgasms.

Problems that can ruin
your sex life can include
illness, drugs, anger,
performance anxiety,
shame and guilt. It cannot
be assumed that a sexual
problem is synonymous with
an unhappy marriage. Few
couples have trouble-free
sex lives.

Treatment for premature ejaculation has dramatically improved the outlook for men who climax too fast. The cure rate approaches 100%, with an average of fourteen weeks of treatment.

Between 10 and 20 million American males suffer impotence at some point in their lives. The likelihood of erectile dysfunction increases with age, but is not an inevitable consequence of ageing.

Impotence is not
'all in a man's head'.
About 85% is caused
by disease, particularly
diabetes and heart
conditions that restrict
blood flow.

Erectile dysfunction is also associated with loss of self-esteem, poor self-image, increased anxiety or tension with one's sexual partner, and/or fear and anxiety associated with contracting sexually-transmitted diseases, including AIDS. Other factors such as obesity, poor physical fitness, as well as heavy smoking and drinking can contribute.

Let's talk about it

Why is it that the
most fascinating subject
known to humankind is
the most difficult for a
couple to talk about?

A couple who can pore over house plans by the hour fall silent when faced with talking about their sex lives. People can revert to the most childish ways of sending indirect messages when sex is involved. Tantrums, silence, pouting, irritability and even name-calling.

When a sexual problem is not addressed, it does anything but disappear. It tends to grow in its dimension and impact.

Communication is always worth a try.

Sex, over the years,
invariably changes.
But that doesn't mean
sex dies.

Women in their 30s
start taking more
sexual initiative. . . .

When women
manifest a new
interest in sex, it
can be the worst
or best phase in
a couple's sex life.

As 40-something women complete the reproductive years, there is a tremendous freedom in realising more fulfilling sex. . . .

The 50s can be relaxed, romantic and intimate. This is when partners are most likely to be perfectly matched sexually and emotionally.

By failing to create an atmosphere in which his wife can respond sexually, a man can deprive himself of the pleasure that is important to his happiness. When things are out of balance in the sexual department, the husband should look at himself for an explanation as to why he has a lukewarm wife.

How to satisfy a woman sexually?

- Romance her *outside* the bedroom first. A woman is stimulated by the amount of romantic love her husband has shown for her throughout the day. Romance her with loving touches, pats and hugs. Hold hands in the car or while you are out walking.

- Spend time in loving foreplay. Don't be a hurry-up lover.

- Understand female pleasure zones.

- Learn to extend love-play. A man can learn to control the point of ejaculation.

- Enter by invitation. A husband should wait until his wife's emotional response matches her physical response.

A woman does not have to achieve an orgasm every time in order to enjoy sex. Many women can participate in sexual relations, not achieve orgasm, and yet feel fully satisfied.

A man who insists on a brief nighttime romp regardless of his wife's mood or her state of health will always end up disappointed in the quality of their sex life.

One of the key factors in achieving a great sex life is remaining committed to one partner. It's called fidelity. Confining sex exclusively to one's partner for a lifetime is the only way to build an emotionally healthy, stable relationship.

'Each one of you should know how to possess (control, manage) his own body in consecration (purity, separated from things profane), and in honour.'
1 Thessalonians 4:4,
Amplified Version.

Self-control is the key ingredient in all sexual expression.

Husbands and wives should aim to be imaginative, creative and willing lovers. God designed that sex – unhampered by selfishness – be exciting, enjoyable and fulfilling.